Deep Surface Fissures Revealing
a Furious Molten Core...

Deep Surface Fissures Revealing a Furious Molten Core...

Hosho McCreesh

Ternary Editions
New York

Deep Surface Fissures © 2018 by Hosho McCreesh

All rights reserved. No part of this text may be used of reproduced in any manner whatsoever without permission from the author, except in the case of brief quotations embodied in critical articles and reviews.

Acknowledgements
The author and publisher would like to thank the following brave, understaffed, underfunded, & underappreciated publications where some of the included work first appeared: *American Dissident, Gnome,* & *Monkey's Fist.*

The first edition of this book was published in 2002 by Stonehenge Studios (Albuquerque, NM) in an edition that was limited to 50 copies.

SECOND PRINTING

ISBN: 978-1-937073-78-7

Ternary Editions
29 Sugar Hill Road
North Salem, NY 10560

ternaryeditions.com

For Dylan Oaks

CONTENTS

When All We Truly Need Is...	1
A Gut-Laugh For...	3
The Sun Will Burn Itself Out	4
Acres Of Tulips In/Screaming	5
On What To Do With/Sunflowers & Scars...	6
10,000ft Thunderheads	7
Insomnia or A Few Scratched-out Lines	9
With A Straight Fucking Face...	12
As The Dim Heavens & Stars/ Bear/ Witness...	13
Dwindling Like Hope...	14
It's Getting Harder & Harder To Believe	16
Stare Up Into The Blue Ice of Night	17
A Quiet, Forgotten Village	19
A Butterfly Flaps Its Wings In Reykjavik	21
As WWII In Europe Ended	22
On How Much We	23
Deep Surface Fissures	24
Ourselves & No One Else...	26
It's Easier To Hear The	27
One For The People Who Think	31
Impossible Petals,/ Drowning In	32
& The World Is A Cold, Hard Place	35
Solitude...	36
The Goddamned Night Presses Down	37
Start With What You Have	38
An Out, An Answer, A Way To	41
As The Leaves Stretch Out,	43
For Centuries Man Has/ Confused	46
How	47
As The Lunatics Scratch	48
Because Van Gogh Didn't Sit	50
Shatter Diamonds Into	51
On A Night Where Nothing	52
Between The Raw Sting	53
Another Gunshot Night...	54
First Rainfall of Spring, 11:57pm	55
The Ghosts &/ Billie Holiday	57
It's Easy; As Easy As Reaching Up	58
One For Those Who Refuse	59

Clouds Smothering the
Incandescent
Heavens,
& The Lot of Us
Leaning Against
Damnation.

When All We Truly Need Is Our Deathmarch Road To Be Lined With Screaming Orange Blossoms...

The dreary eternity of
here to
there,
fiery cinders raining down
through the cold & the
wet
while we spend
      hours
      sunsets
      stone carved nights
      birth & deaths of stars
waiting,
waiting, &
waiting
for something,
anything—
we don't even know what,
just that we don't
have it.

You know, & I know,
we all fucking know—
we know we've been
bamboozled...
told it was
courage
that kept us at the job we hate
when we know it's
fear
& only fear
that keeps the structure

propped up on the bent backs of the
dead & dying.

They need you
afraid.
They need you
eyes forward, in line, &
knifing your fellow man for personal gain.
They need you
afraid of
possibilities.
They need you as a productive
member of a society that otherwise
couldn't
care
less.

We know this.

& knowing,
now there is
no feasible
excuse.

A Gut-Laugh For The Heavens & The Gods...

In theory
we
as a species
are moving
forward...

...yet we
        design
           manufacture
           & install
bus stop benches
that prevent
the homeless
from
sleeping
on
them.

```
The Sun Will Burn Itself Out,
& An Apocalyptic, Hellish Winter Will Set In
& Kill Almost Everything On This Silly Rock
& Anything That Remains Can Wait Patiently
For The Universe To Collapse Back Onto Itself...
```

…the very first,
most basic
victory
is accepting
—without fear or doubt—
that you
will
die
& that a
gravestone
is a pathetic,
sorry-ass
excuse
for a
legacy.

There,
that should make
the rest
much
easier.

```
Acres Of Tulips In
Screaming Full Bloom
Yet Burning Under
New-fallen Snow...
```

The gods say
nothing—

—either they
cannot
or they
chose
not to.

Whatever the case,
it leaves us
to us, to our
paperclips &
best guesses
& so, if you think
what you are doing
actually
matters,
if you think the gods
will applaud your
imminent arrival,
then perhaps you're
getting it
right…

But make
no
mistake,

most

don't.

**On What To Do With
Sunflowers & Scars...**

There's
real, actual
beauty
doled out in
tiny little
rations
& then there's
the full-on
savagery
of the
human
animal...

...very little
actually
matters.

So if it
does matter,
put it
where it
belongs—
>   locked deep away or
>   in a goddamned poem.

Keep it
or let it go...

Either way
don't worry
too much
about it..

rarely
will it
outlive
you.

```
10,000ft Thunderheads That
Grumble & Crackle, Are
Ripped Apart By Lightning
& Then
Erupt &
Spill...
```

No poems tonight & goodgoddamn
on nights like these
it just ain't enough to
rip at yourself with a jagged, rusted blade or
strip down to your shorts &
start sucking on beers.

It all just hangs around like tulips,
heavy & full-up with rain,
the nightmare of it all—
        tangled people, quiet in beds & bedrooms,
        blue TVs flickering through living room blinds,
        plane crashes,
        divorces,
        falling in love,
        stinking, brittle socks, or
        10,000ft thunderheads that
        grumble & crackle, are
        ripped apart by lightning
        & then
        erupt &
        spill...

& you just can't get the beers down fast enough.

Oh, to find a way,
to get the ugliness to go,
even if only for a while...

...but the walls just stand there,
holding each other up,
silent as gravestones

& the people, they're gravestones too
& it's all just nothing,
nothing & nothing &
more
nothing
after that.

So I take 3 oil-rigger gulps,
3 greedy swallows,
finish off a bottle,
go the to fridge for
another, thinking,
To hell with these nights.
To hell with all of this
shit…

& quietly search for a way,
my way,
some sort of trick to get
outside myself
& again find
beauty
in what
remains.

Insomnia...
-or-
A Few Scratched-out Lines For Perverts & Birds, For Flowers & Soldiers & Traffic Lights, For Nuclear Warheads, & Mothers, & Communists & For The Running Of The Bulls In Pamplona...

It's a rough one tonight.

Even more so than usual—
like something sinewy,
meaty & blood-ripped,
twitching in the mouth of a
kestrel,
like poppies folding up their petals
to the impending
storm…

I should be asleep.

But I just can't help thinking
the best & brightest are
raging angels sniffing glue
& the rest just stand there like
telephone poles &
streetlights &
traffic signals—
only interesting if they don't work or are
without power or are
burnt out, only noticed when they don't do what is
expected, don't do what they're
supposed to
& all the while
tactical nuclear warheads
slant & slouch & slope,
mapping out a trajectory across the drunk, burning heavens
Beijing to Washington D.C. & back again
& no one cares much, they just race home to

horrible sitcoms & husbands & wives they no longer love
& I remember thirteen Thursdays ago the guy next to me in
rush hour gridlock thumbing through a porno mag &
that was a particularly beautiful afternoon
& I'll probably miss the running of the bulls in Pamplona again next year
but I bet you can still find mushroomed-out bullets
in the sands of Normandy,
& that's really something—
spent shells uncovered by torrential rain, & the thick musk
of dead young men's blood dangling brown &
effervescent in the sea foam.

We are all outnumbered,
like that pigeon, face down in the gutter,
wings splayed—
dead but still
grasping at life,
we're ripped up & across, torn at, fed on & gouged out,
we're Rommel's panzer tracks across the sands of Egypt
& in Wisconsin there's a mother of 3 with a hysterectomy
& Phlebitis in her left leg who works in a factory 8 hours day
(less if she can get away with it, sneaking cigarettes
behind the foreman's billboard forehead, his pin-prick eyes
because she's convinced the world owes her something,
it must otherwise she wouldn't always feel so empty...)
& she makes the bullets that one day will be
fired by trembling teenage patriots &
pierce pregnant stomachs & work-bent spines of
dusty backed 3rd world farmers wielding rakes & spades,
a revolution deep down in their bone marrow,
& the anchorman will tell us that they were
Communists & terrorists
& not just hungry people & that'll make everything
okay...

It really is a rough one tonight.

Even more so than usual.

I really should
just get some
sleep...

With A Straight Fucking Face...

...the Hollywood starlet
speaks of
sacrifice...

I think of
all that has been
sacrificed
just to get us
this
chance—

what early man had to
      eat
      discover
      decipher
      endure
just so we'd
be
here.

I think of acts of god:
      plague, famine, drought,
      tsunami, tornado, fire, quake—
      all manner of
      natural
      savagery.

& worse, the
immeasurably brutal acts of
man.

& this is
all
we've
done
with
it.

```
As The Dim Heavens & Stars
Bear
Witness...
```

3:38am
& again the
cops,
two houses down,
the front picture window
smashed
—splintered diamonds swept off to the neglected dirt yard—
teenage mother crying
as the dim heavens & stars
bear
witness...

By morning
plywood
covering the screaming, jagged-toothed hole &
by afternoon
the little girls
returning home from school, afraid of
another imminent nightfall,
dreaming of
escape &
places that know
only flooding
yellow
sunshine...

The cops
write another report
& leave.

Dwindling Like Hope...

Our personal
suffering
is necessary yet
insignificant
when compared to the
sheer, unsurpassed
originality
of a hunched-over & inspired
ancestor
when they
first
picked up a stone &
used it as a
tool—
the stone becoming
a blade & hammer, a way to
splinter
the picked-clean bones
& get at the rich, fatty,
necessary
marrow,
& then there's the first to take a
charcoaled tree limb
to a pale, blank
cave wall,
which became
      a paintbrush
      a narrative
      a kind of evidence & meaning...

& since then, only
one thing has
suffered
more than
ART, dwindling like hope as the
human animal
"progressed"

to where we
currently
find
ourselves:

        everything that
        existed
        before
        us.

It's Getting Harder & Harder To Believe That Weapons Grade Plutonium, Tit Pills, & The Ghosts In Our Pasts Matter Much...

At our best
we live life to
our very
edges.

At our worst, we
do things
just to say we've been
doing things,
just in case someone
asks.

But you can't get a decent glass of
lemonade anymore
& the devil sits at a greasy spoon diner in
Kingman, Arizona, the kind with pictures
of guys in camouflage smiling,
holding up, by the antlers, the animals they've killed.
The devil just sits there,
reading the Washington Post,
cackling at all he's done,
the preposterous brutality of living,
his pants unbuttoned because his breakfast has settled—
      the blue plate special: steak & eggs for $4.95, coffee,
      & a slice of peach pie because he was
      famished from the previous night's
      country & western
      line dancing—

& it's plain to see
that we, all of us,
we have
been
forgotten.

```
Stare Up Into The Blue Ice Of Night,
At The Ruptured-Blister Stars
Amidst The Report & Echo Of Gunshots,
& Know—Not Think—KNOW, That None Of It Matters,
Nothing Cosmic Cares About You Or Me Or The Little
Screaming Faces On Light Sockets...
```

There's definitely too much
doom
in the sky,
the stars,
to just sit back &
take it
all.

But we
must, we have
no choice.

Believe what you chose to
believe—
       life after death
       a divine purpose, plan
       a deity with a
       heaven, a hell, or a
       Kentucky Fried Chicken—
nothing changes the fact that
nothing beyond our
very immediate,
very limited reach
cares about
us—
not as individuals,
members of a nation, or the
8 (supposedly) important economic nations,
not as humans, or even as a part of the
discernable life on this planet...

Know that
before you
decide
what matters
most.

& knowing that,
do what you
want
be what you
want...

Be
        tailors
        research assistants
        bartenders
        custodians or
        a guy who makes enormous neon & metal signs...

It makes
no sense
not
to.

```
A Quiet, Forgotten Village In The
Swiss Alps, The Whole Place
Reduced To Smoldering Ash & Hot
Blood Melting Through Snow...
```

"That's right," she said,
"it is all such a
crapshoot…"

We were drinking margaritas
in an okay bar
with lousy art on its walls
overlooking a rainy Oregon cove,
& we talked about calla lilies & the
dumb, blind courage of
marriage, & of
living in
general…

"We know 3 couples
in the last few years
who've divorced
after over 20 years
together."

& there are terrible stories, awful stories,
just as there are terrible, awful
      rainstorms,
      droughts, &
      armies thundering the cadence of destruction
      through cobblestone streets, as they
      loot & rape & plunder & then torch
      a quiet, forgotten village in the
      Swiss Alps, the whole place
      reduced to smoldering ash & hot
      blood melting through snow…

monstrous stories,
& there will be again—

mankind is
nothing
if not
predictable.

Horrible stories, the world is full of them,
too full of them:
    —a guy kills his family with a $100 meat cleaver & dumps them in the bay…
    —another guy gets drunk & kills himself in the garage after a fight with his girl, who woke to a noise but then fell back asleep in the near-by bedroom…
    —a wife wakes in the middle of the night to find her husband dead & not knowing who to call or what to do with herself, she just goes back to sleep…
    —people together for 13 months, 37 years, or 7 decades finally give in, a slow, quiet kind of trauma…

& what is remarkable
yet constantly ignored
isn't
that it hardly ever works out,
but that it sometimes,
(rarely but occasionally)
does…

& if it does,
or if it doesn't,
even still
we all
manage,
we all
find a way to
somehow
continue.

A Butterfly Flaps Its Wings In Reykjavik &
One Guy Gets Filthy Rich While The Other
Ends Up Weeping Uncontrollably
Among Rats & Broken Bottles
In A Squalid Alley
Alone...

It is simultaneously horrific & divine,
all the things humans can do—
the way so little actually separates
the earthworm from the king,
the drunk from the genius,
madmen from millionaires.
It can sometimes be traced back to a
moment:
> a butterfly flaps its wings in Reykjavik &
> one guy gets filthy rich while the other ends up
> weeping uncontrollably among rats & broken bottles
> in a squalid alley
> alone...

But we're left, instead, to
all we have, all we've done, which is
laughable & isn't much
while the earth is overrun
by these locusts,
by unimaginative drivel,
by clutter,
by spent oxygen tanks & frozen Texan's bodies
sprinkled like bright red candy atop Everest,
almost no untouched place
exists—

—& there will never be a fire
extravagant & substantial enough to
save us.

As WWII In Europe Ended,
They Said Hitler Was Mad Because
He Ordered The Destruction Of All Of Paris
As His Stranglehold On France Slipped,
But The Allies Bombed Dresden Into
Toothpicks & Gravel Despite It Holding
No Viable Military Significance.

It is
unforgivable
to, in the interest of an
imagined
solidarity,
turn a blind eye to
brutality, any
brutality—

—especially our
own.

```
On How Much We Chose To Leave The Buzzards,
The Jackals, & The Worms...
```

Rarely do they ever
take from us
anything
we didn't
readily
give…

It happens, sure,
but not nearly as much
as we like to
pretend.

We entomb ourselves—
buying all their
      bullshit bells & whistles
      mystical snake oils
      thingamajigs
      dohickies
      whatchamabobs
by believing their lies,
believing we should
wait to
live
well.

To find
      truth
      meaning
      beauty
that's why we're
here…

…that &
no other
reason.

**Deep Surface Fissures
Revealing A Furious
Molten Core...**

Clouds smothering the
incandescent
heavens,
& the lot of us
leaning against
damnation.

Coughing in gridlock,
going places, doing things
that truly
do
not
matter.

The spirit
remains
caged—
      deep surface fissures
      revealing a furious
      molten core...

Something internal
begs us;
escape,
run from this,
break free of
this—

—but most just turn a
deaf
ear
& continue on,
suffering
without partaking in their

suffering,
without
acknowledge-
ment.

They deny it
like they deny the
truth—

> a
> rotting carcass
> & the 5 buzzards
> drifting,
> swirling
> on a thermal
> updraft
> above
> it.

—most
simply
chose
not
to.

Ourselves & No One Else...

...we are the
only
ones
who should
decide
whether or
not
we
are
failures.

```
It's Easier To Hear The
Breathing Cosmos At Night,
The Shrill
Scream
Of No
Noise...
```

We're mostly fools
schlepping around,
believing all the
shit
we
believe—

It's mostly just the
shivering cold, the
defeat of
lifelong
routine
out there
waiting
for almost
everyone—

—mostly.

Something Internal
Begs Us;
Run From This,
Break Free of
This—

One For The People Who Think It's Easy To Write Poems, & For Those Who Think Poems About Ex-Lovers Actually Matter...

Heard a story once about a guy who was
attacked by something
wild
& the thing gored & eviscerated him
& he literally had to drag his guts
through the woods
to a road, miles away,
& collapse.

A pair of headlights
would find him later,
& in the emergency room
they couldn't sedate him,
they were afraid he was too weak to survive it,
that they couldn't revive him if they did,
so they hand-washed his intestines,
scrubbed away the
      grit
      pebbles
      twigs
      pine needles
him wide awake & watching
feeling it
all
full-bore, &
straight on
through...

He lived.

Now that's a
goddamned
poem.

```
Impossible Petals,
Drowning In Their Own
Impossible Color,
Their Palms Raised Up
In A Quiet Offering...
```

for Roybal, & Us Too...

It was a different time then,
just after one of my best friends
died.

I was, again,
stunted
by a kind of
silent
insanity—

—had to really
concentrate
on just
going
on
despite
everything.

When it's nothing but
savage dark
ruling the day
it makes it
damn near
impossible
to see a
way
out.

So you rely on
routine—
      get up
      brush teeth

    meet daily obligations
    return home
    eat something
    brush teeth (because even though
    you might not have much,
    you've somehow managed not to
    abandon all hope of sunshine
    & the uncorrupted kind of screaming yellow
    paint dragged across a blank canvas &
    you haven't given up on tomorrow either)
    sleep
    repeat until it no longer hurts
    to be
    held.

& there's something to be said for
surviving it,
just like you
survived
        the fire
        the physical domination
        the cancers
        the looks while paying with food stamps
        the swindle…

Yes, those were different times.

So now it's easy,
well, no; Easier—
now I can sometimes just
sit &
marvel
at it all,
still not much closer to
any kind of relaxing sigh,
no closer to escaping the innumerable pits,
but we've somehow kept out the

cold
& we've
rebuilt.

& here we still are,
still smiling,
the one thing
we could
always do,
the one thing
all of it could
never
get.

& The World Is A Cold, Hard Place
But Not As Unforgiving As A Tomb,
So Tear Away The Incessant Deception
Until Only The Following Remains...

Get only what
you
need.

Ignore the
rest—
all of
it.

& now do something
beautiful,
do that one thing
you
always
said
you'd
do.

Solitude...

...is it's own kind of
smiling
reward...

& it usually takes a
lifetime
to know
it.

```
The Goddamned Night Presses Down
Like Cement As I Quietly Ponder
What The Future Holds
Should I
Fail...
```

Another night filled with
gunshots & screams
& here we are, making all kinds of
decisions
that will, in 50 years,
no doubt, land us in a
desperate place,
maybe without even a bed to
die
in—

—but everything inside me says
this is right,
even though the
gods
only give us guesses &
the dizzy, swarming
wasps
of failure,
maybe a few successes mixed in,
all droning on & on through some
wet summer air
as we all just
sit down
under our naked 60 watt
to yet
another
empty page &
bet
on
our-
selves.

Start With What You Have & Like
Shark Attacks, Lightning Strikes, &
Death—
It Makes No Sense To
Dwell
On It...

28 cents & a dislocated shoulder—
& they all have places to go,
places to forget the
hum-drum
savagery of
man (if they even notice it)
  hockey games
  titty bars
  the office
  take the dog for a walk
  fuck some mistress or
  buy roses for their wives.

We have no place to go.

Elephants with their tusks sawed off
know better,
& sharks with their dorsal fins
loped off—
because some crackpot somewhere once said
it may help maintain an
erection—
know better than
we
do.

Where can we go?
To get clear of all this?
  Saint Louis?
  The Ukraine?
  The Kassol Passage in Palau?
  Further in the universe

than man has ever seen,
dreamed of or
imagined?

It will do no good.
It will do no good because
somewhere an old widower is
clipping coupons
from a newspaper advertisement
& she will
die
before she can
use
them,
& the madhouses of America
should be jammed full, bursting at the seams
& every incarcerated gullet should be
repeatedly packed with
tripe
for all the
blasé
savagery
we've
deliberately
ignored
as the plastic grocery bags of
surrender
caught in powerlines & winter tree limbs
hiss & ker-lap
& the streets still drink gallon after gallon of
hot, senseless blood
& only a weary few remain,
running further
& further
from the
American
Dream—

—the dignity of
those lives
silently climbing the walls
up into a corner like a
brown
recluse.

An Out, An Answer, A Way To Hold Off The Savage Dark As It Presses Down On All Of Us Like All The World's Interconnected Oceans Press Down On The Mariana Trench...

Almost all is
sacrifice.

Almost all is the
doing of what
must
be
done
while we patiently
wait
to do
what
we
must.

So,
when you do
get a
chance,
do work
that
matters—

—& leave it here to be
forgotten &
rediscovered, to be
trapped in an
airtight
pocket
amongst the
rubble &
twisted metal
of the
end,

perfectly preserved &
waiting on the
future...

Then & only then
will the
sacrifice
have been
worth
it.

As The Leaves Stretch Out,
Tirelessly Reaching For
Sunlight,
As The Piercing Stars
Drill Down,
Bolting Us To It...

There is no grace tonight.

Tonight it's all
unfair.

It seems every single
tiny little
taste
we get is
punished,
as if we
owe some
cosmic
debt
for brief moments of
effortless, smiling
joy.

It's times like these we
witness
the impenetrable
magnitude of the
structure,
how completely it's
turned
like a screwhead
against
us—
only there to
continue
supporting
itself.

We see, clearly,
that we can
never
win…

…& so our question, then,
is can we
continue
despite
that,
as the leaves stretch out,
tirelessly reaching for
sunlight,
as the piercing stars
drill down,
bolting us to it
& even though we
probably
don't
want
to,

we
have
to,

we
must—

we have to
dig out
sapphires—
drag them from their
prison-soil,
dig out a little more
strength,
expose a little more

meaning
where
none
currently
exists.

There is
simply
no other
way.

For Centuries Man Has
Confused
The Obliteration Of
Beauty
As Accomplishment Or Conquest...

...it's in the way Hitler
abandoned painting for
genocide,
it's the incurable
frustration of being
incomplete as
humans.

We often find ourselves
struggling
against any kind of
happiness—

which is
foolish.

It will all
kill
us
soon
enough.

Laugh at &
willingly accept
as much as
possible—

all the
good stuff...

...& all the
rest too.

How

Realize that
nothing
can be
beautiful by
trying,
nothing
can be
beautiful on
purpose,
then beat the cold stone walls
'til the bones of your hands
turn to
powder,
out crack the purple
thundering
heavens,
tear a hole in the
blackest
night
& claw through it
to the
pure
white
light of
nothing.

As The Lunatics Scratch At Pale, Dingy Walls With A Splintered, Bloody Fingertip...

To do what we can—
that's admirable.

To shave away portions of it
until a deeper, hidden core is
revealed,
as the lunatics scratch at pale, dingy walls
with a splintered, bloody
fingertip, & we
gather the night like
wildflowers,
wield it with the
magnitude of the
heavens.

Scream at the moon 'til it shatters.

Disown the sun.

Built it up as you'd
have
it—
embrace the
swirling
fury
of the
ignored
cosmos
as the walls just stand there,
& the windows just hold most of it out,
& the coalsmoke night sits on us all like
      a violation
      a pathogen
      a brutal regime,

& the naked bulb, at this angle,
shoots out gritty, texture shadows
across the
scream of
night,
while we sit,
refusing to
relent,
insisting that some
beauty
must
endure.

Because Van Gogh Didn't Sit In The Asylum
Waiting For Starry Night To Paint Itself,
Because Michelangelo Didn't Sit In Florence
Waiting For The Pieta To Carve Itself...

It takes
years
for tree limbs to
tear down
powerlines,
for roots to
buckle
concrete...

...but they
always
do.

Shatter Diamonds Into Shrapnel, Shards & Dust...

It's a kind of
celebration,
the dirt & blood
under fingernails
as we push for it,
thrash through it
grab those close enough &
drag them along with us because
we have managed to keep our feet &
they've briefly stumbled.

All we can do is
our part—
shatter diamonds into
shrapnel, shards &
dust
while the steamroller of these
apocalyptic badlands
gathers speed &
grows like the
burbs &
somehow cats sleep in chairs &
the universe again goes silent &
we switch out the light on
another day,
another night
unsquandered.

On A Night Where Nothing Much Happened;
I Listened To Some Music While
Writing My Brother A 7 Pg Letter
& For Whatever Reason The Heavens
Cracked Open
& The Gods Riotously Applauded
& Later, As I Nodded Off To Sleep,
The Dead Kept Repeating My Name...

There shall be
no apologies
for a night
like
tonight...

...because I just don't think
you get too many
like this
in an
entire
life-
time.

Between The Raw Sting & The Dull Ache,
Between Antibiotics & The Splitting of Atoms,
Between All That Has Been & All That Will Be
Again...

...there's deep breaths of
cool, damp
air,
the desert
after
rain.

There's sunlight.

There's a star
long dead
that still
shines
for
us
to
see.

& there's
us,
still alive
to
see
it
all.

Another Gunshot Night...

...wads up like a
fist
& the ambulances scream,
carrying half-eaten sandwiches &
slabs of mangled folks—
spiraling as it
writhes in the ears,
their last
earthly
wail—

& then there's the poems,
the little
outnumbered
poems
thundering,
cackling like madmen,
beating the pale walls
& it's

them

vs.

all the
rest.

First Rainfall Of Spring, 11:57pm

The streets
hiss
& the
gutters
run over.

Budding branches
scratch
at the
sinking
heavens.

There's
liquid
staccato.

Sheets of it
stomp
like Hitler's troops in
'38 as the
muffled
stars
never stop trying to
scream
through the
rainsoaked
midnight.

I stand in it
with my shirt
off
& let it
all
drain.

The Ghosts &
Billie Holiday &
Dead Baby Sparrows...

Sadness hangs in the drunk air tonight
like bar smoke in clothes
—full through & permeated—
like the smell of burning weeds in late winter,
as I listen to Billie Holiday & say to the
ghosts
"Okay, you win...
tonight, you
win..."

I'm remember Aberdeen, Scotland
years back,
& my daily routine
took me past
a dead baby sparrow
3 different times by
noon.

A 4th time would've been
too
much...
I just couldn't keep
walking by
pretending not to
care.

Gripping twigs like
chopsticks,
I swatted at the flies,
awkwardly picked it up, &
carried it off to a
quiet, untrampled
place.

& after burying that
dead baby sparrow
    because it's all that seemed fair
    because it's the only thing that seemed right
    because I could not pass it up once more
    because I could not watch the flies
    taunt & wander his tiny, perfect little
    carcass & I just couldn't
    understand
    why beautiful things had to
    die
    too
I twisted some wire
around the 2 twigs,
fashioned an inadequate
cross
to mark the
grave.

I felt like crying.

I laughed
instead.

**It's Easy; As Easy As Reaching Up &
Crushing The Sun In Your
Fist, Devouring It,
Letting It Blister
Your
Insides...**

...it's all as
simple
or as
complicated
as we
make
it.

One For Those Who Refuse, Who Search, For Those Who See Through It All & Beyond...

Milling through
ripped
pockets
searching for a
chance,
& all we find is
a dizzy ravel of
ignorant craving &
stinging failure—
yep, that seems to be
about the
trudge
of it.

We are
quashed
by our
raw, turgid
comforts,
forgetting
that we're just the
fossils of
tomorrow.

What we need is a
catalyst—
a blade of
light
knifing through the
hot, woolen black
while this world
drunk on
    wealth
    greed
    power

stumbles unwittingly into the
apocalypse,
a drooling, stupid
smile on its
face.

Distill.

Filtrate.

Draw out the
essence—
built it
with fat, fearless
brushwork
& climb it like a
tomb…

…singing in the

drunk, splintered

sunlight.

Photograph © 2018 by Freddy De La Cruz

About the Author

Hosho McCreesh lives, writes, works, and paints in the gypsum and caliche badlands of the American Southwest. The best way to follow his work is via his website: www.hoshomccreesh.com

COLOPHON

Deep Surface Fissures Revealing a Furious Molten Core... was designed by Bill Roberts and published by Ternary Editions in June 2018. The text is set in Adobe Caslon Pro with My Underwood as the titling font.

www.ingramcontent.com/pod-product-compliance
Lightning Source LLC
Chambersburg PA
CBHW071315060426
42444CB00036B/3030